W9-BSB-847

EXPLORING COUNTRIES

Ethiopia

by Ellen Frazel

BELLWETHER MEDIA · MINNEAPOLIS, MN

Note to Librarians, Teachers, and Parents:

Blastoff! Readers are carefully developed by literacy experts and combine standards-based content with developmentally appropriate text.

Level 1 provides the most support through repetition of high-frequency words, light text, predictable sentence patterns, and strong visual support.

Level 2 offers early readers a bit more challenge through varied simple sentences, increased text load, and less repetition of high-frequency words.

Level 3 advances early-fluent readers toward fluency through increased text and concept load, less reliance on visuals, longer sentences, and more literary language.

Level 4 builds reading stamina by providing more text per page, increased use of punctuation, greater variation in sentence patterns, and increasingly challenging vocabulary.

Level 5 encourages children to move from "learning to read" to "reading to learn" by providing even more text, varied writing styles, and less familiar topics.

Whichever book is right for your reader, Blastoff! Readers are the perfect books to build confidence and encourage a love of reading that will last a lifetime!

This edition first published in 2013 by Bellwether Media, Inc.

No part of this publication may be reproduced in whole or in part without written permission of the publisher. For information regarding permission, write to Bellwether Media, Inc., Attention: Permissions Department, 5357 Penn Avenue South, Minneapolis, MN 55419.

Library of Congress Cataloging-in-Publication Data
Frazel, Ellen.
  Ethiopia / by Ellen Frazel.
    p. cm. – (Blastoff! readers: Exploring countries)
  Includes bibliographical references and index.
  Summary: "Developed by literacy experts for students in grades three through seven, this book introduces young readers to the geography and culture of Ethiopia"–Provided by publisher.
  ISBN 978-1-60014-859-0 (hardcover : alk. paper)
  1. Ethiopia–Juvenile literature. I. Title. II. Series: Blastoff! readers. 5, Exploring countries.
  DT373.F74 2013
  963–dc23   2012030661

Printed in the United States of America, North Mankato, MN.

Contents

Where Is Ethiopia?   4
The Land   6
The Danakil Desert   8
Wildlife   10
The People   12
Daily Life   14
Going to School   16
Working   18
Playing   20
Food   22
Holidays   24
Aksum and Lalibela   26
Fast Facts   28
Glossary   30
To Learn More   31
Index   32

Ethiopia is a **landlocked** country in East Africa. Sudan and South Sudan border Ethiopia to the west. Eritrea and Djibouti are its neighbors to the north. Somalia stretches along the eastern border, and Kenya lies to the south.

Ethiopia covers 426,373 square miles (1,104,300 square kilometers). It makes up a large part of the **Horn of Africa**. Ethiopia's capital, Addis Ababa, is located in the center of the country.

Sudan

South Sudan

4

Eritrea

Red
Sea

Djibouti

Addis Ababa ★

Ethiopia

Somalia

Kenya

Indian
Ocean

Did you know?
Ethiopia is one of the first places where early humans existed on Earth. Fossils that date back 6 million years have been discovered there.

N
W E
S

Did you know?

The Ethiopian Highlands are sometimes called the "Roof of Africa" because of their height and the large area that they cover.

Blue Nile River

fun fact

Ethiopia has a tropical monsoon climate. It rains lightly from February to April and then heavily from the middle of June to the middle of September.

Ethiopia has many different landscapes. Mountains and **plateaus** rise through much of central Ethiopia. This region is called the Ethiopian Highlands. It is divided in half from the northeast to the southwest by the Great Rift Valley. The highlands slope into lowlands that reach to the borders of the country.

In the northeast, little to no rain falls on the Danakil Desert. **Tropical rain forests** can be found in the south. In the north, the Blue Nile River flows out of Lake Tana. The weather is usually cooler in the highlands and hotter on the coasts.

7

The Danakil Desert

The Danakil Desert is considered one of the most unlivable places on Earth. This hot, dry land sweeps across northeastern Ethiopia and into Eritrea and Djibouti. It is home to the Danakil **Depression**, one of the hottest places in the world.

The land dips as low as 410 feet (125 meters) below **sea level** in the Danakil Depression. This region holds Erta Ale **volcano**, where lava bubbles and spews hot gases. In Dallol volcano, **hot springs** bring saltwater to the surface. The water dries up, leaving colorful fields of salt. With its scorching heat, fiery lava, and bright landscapes, the Danakil Desert is like an entirely different planet.

Erta Ale

Did you know?

Green acid salt ponds can be found throughout Dallol. Salt builds up in these ponds to form structures that look like fluffy orange cakes.

Did you know?
The saddlebill stork is a huge bird that lives in Ethiopia. It can grow to be almost 5 feet (1.5 meters) tall!

Many animals in Ethiopia live in the cooler climate of the highlands. Thick fur keeps the gelada baboon warm in the cold mountains. **Endangered** walia ibex live on the steep, rocky cliffs. Spotted hyenas stalk the ibex through the grass. In the southern highlands, the mountain nyala grazes on grasses and shrubs. Servals and caracals also roam the region.

gelada baboon

caracal

saddlebill stork

nyala

Tilapia and Nile perch swim in the lakes of the Great Rift Valley. Hippopotamuses and crocodiles also lurk in the water. Flocks of pink flamingos, great white pelicans, and long-tailed cormorants fly overhead.

Ethiopia is very **diverse**. Over 91 million people live in the country. About 3 in every 10 are Oromo. The Amhara, Somali, and Tigray are the next largest people groups. Each speaks its own **native** language. People from Eritrea and Sudan have also come to live in Ethiopia. Amharic is the country's official language, but Oromigna and Tigrigna are spoken in certain areas. English and Arabic are the official foreign languages.

Speak Amharic!

English	Amharic	How to say it
hello	selam	seh-LAHM
good-bye	dehna hun	day-na HOON
yes	awo	ah-woh
no	aye	eye
thank you	ameseginalehu	ah-meh-seg-nahl-hoo
please (male)	i'bakih	ih-BAH-keh
please (female)	i'bakish	ih-BAH-kesh
friend	gwadanya	gwah-dehn-yah

fun fact

A few men in Harar perform a dangerous stunt at night. They feed wild hyenas with their bare hands!

Many Ethiopians live like their **ancestors** did. Most people live in the countryside. They build houses out of stones, mud, and wood. Families are large, and everyone helps with daily tasks. Men often spend the day working on the land. Women gather food and prepare meals. Children help by carrying water from wells back to their homes.

In cities, some people live in modern houses and apartments. Many still live in homes made of simple materials like mud and wood. People drive, walk, or take minibuses from place to place.

Where People Live in Ethiopia

cities
17%

countryside
83%

Did you know?
Ethiopians follow their own calendar system. The Ethiopian calendar is seven to eight years behind the calendar used in the United States.

Going to school can be difficult for many children in Ethiopia. Those who live in the countryside must often help with work at home. Many students cannot afford school supplies. Those who do attend begin with eight years of primary school. They learn basic reading, writing, and math.

After this, students take two years of lower secondary school and two years of higher secondary school. They study science, literature, and other advanced subjects that prepare them for university. Students who go on to university may study medicine, law, or other careers.

Where People Work in Ethiopia

farming 85%

services 10%

manufacturing 5%

Most Ethiopians rise early in the morning to begin farm work. They grow coffee beans, cotton, barley, and other crops. Some farmers raise livestock. They tend their sheep, goats, and cattle. Often, the whole family helps out in the field.

Some people work in factories. They make **textiles**, chemicals, and food products. In major cities, many Ethiopians have **service jobs**. They work in banks, hospitals, and other places that serve local people. Some own restaurants or hotels that are popular with **tourists**.

Ethiopians enjoy many fun activities that represent their culture. Native groups like the Oromo and Amhara are known for their music and dancing. Some groups sing traditional music with drums and stringed instruments. People twirl and dance to the beats.

Sports are also popular in Ethiopia. Many people play soccer, but most athletes favor track-and-field. Some of the country's long-distance runners are known around the world.

! **fun fact**

Many Ethiopians have won Olympic gold medals in track-and-field. Oromo athlete Kenenisa Bekele set world records in both the 5,000- and 10,000-meter events.

Did you know?

Goorsha is a common mealtime tradition. One person takes a strip of *injera*, rolls it in *wat*, and then places it in another's mouth. This is a gesture of friendship.

injera

Almost every meal in Ethiopia includes *injera*. People use this sourdough flatbread to scoop up their food. A typical breakfast dish is *firfir*. Shredded pieces of *injera* are seasoned with *berbere*, a mixture of powdered chili pepper and other spices. Throughout the day, people may snack on *kolo*, or roasted barley.

Dinner typically consists of *injera* with different stews, or *wats*. These *wats* are made with chopped red onions, meats, vegetables, and a touch of *berbere*. A cup of honey-sweetened coffee often finishes the meal.

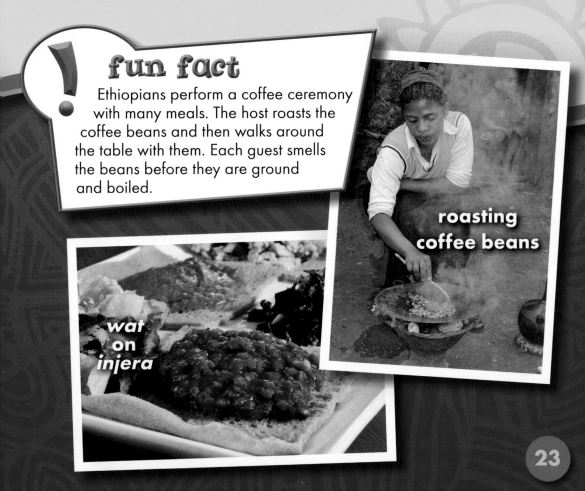

fun fact

Ethiopians perform a coffee ceremony with many meals. The host roasts the coffee beans and then walks around the table with them. Each guest smells the beans before they are ground and boiled.

roasting coffee beans

wat on injera

Many Ethiopians celebrate Christian holidays. *Genna*, or Ethiopian Christmas, is on January 7. People **fast** for forty days and then enjoy feasts on *Genna*. January 19 is *Timkat*, or Epiphany. Crowds gather at rivers and lakes to remember the **baptism** of **Jesus Christ**. Another important religious holiday is *Meskel*, or the Finding of the True Cross. Priests dressed in bright robes march down the streets with flaming torches.

New Year's Day falls on September 11 in Ethiopia. This also marks the end of the rainy season. May 28 is Ethiopia's National Day. It honors the day in 1991 that ended several years of military rule in Ethiopia. People visit **monuments** and listen to speeches about their country.

Did you know?
Some Ethiopians are Muslim. They celebrate Ramadan and other Islamic holidays.

Timkat

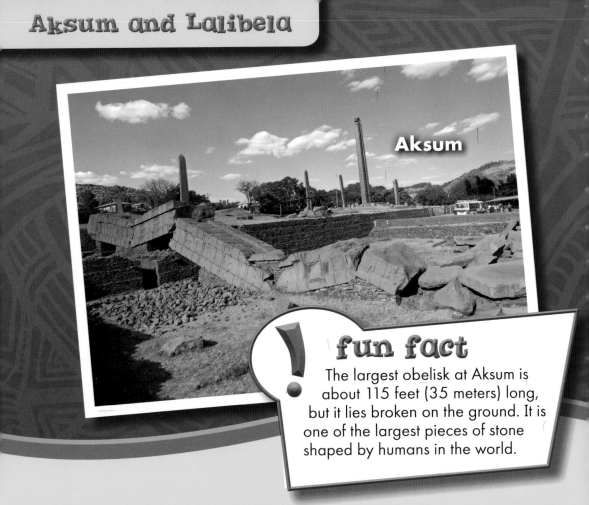

Aksum

! fun fact

The largest obelisk at Aksum is about 115 feet (35 meters) long, but it lies broken on the ground. It is one of the largest pieces of stone shaped by humans in the world.

Aksum and Lalibela are two holy cities in Ethiopia. Built around 400 BCE, Aksum is the oldest city in the country. It is a holy city for both Christians and Muslims. The city is known for its giant **obelisks** and ancient **artifacts**. The Ezana Stone holds ancient carvings that describe the history of the Kingdom of Aksum.

In Lalibela, there are large churches built out of single blocks of stone. Many Christians make a **pilgrimage** to Lalibela to see these churches. The beautiful artifacts of Aksum and Lalibela remind Ethiopians of the long, unique history that brings them together as a people.

Did you know?
One church in Lalibela contains the Lalibela Cross. This cross dates back to the 1100s and is considered one of Ethiopia's most valued religious artifacts.

Fast Facts About Ethiopia

Ethiopia's Flag

The flag of Ethiopia has three horizontal bands. The green band on top is a symbol of hope and the land. In the middle, yellow stands for harmony and justice. The red band at the bottom represents the sacrifices Ethiopians have made to defend their land. A blue circle with a yellow star sits in the middle of the flag. The color blue stands for peace, and the star represents the unity and equality of the Ethiopian people.

Official Name: Federal Democratic Republic of Ethiopia

Area: 426,373 square miles (1,104,300 square kilometers); Ethiopia is the 27th largest country in the world.

Capital City:	Addis Ababa
Important Cities:	Mekele, Adama, Dire Dawa, Gonder
Population:	91,195,675 (July 2012)
Official Languages:	Amharic, Oromigna, Tigrigna, English, Arabic
National Holiday:	National Day (May 28)
Religions:	Christian (62.8%), Muslim (33.9%), traditional beliefs (2.6%), other (0.7%)
Major Industries:	farming, services
Natural Resources:	gold, hydropower
Manufactured Products:	textiles, chemicals, leather, cement, food products
Farm Products:	grains, coffee beans, cotton, sugarcane, livestock, fish
Unit of Money:	birr; the birr is divided into 100 santims.

Glossary

ancestors—relatives who lived long ago

artifacts—items made by humans hundreds of years ago

baptism—a Christian ceremony that uses water to purify a person and welcome him or her into the Church

depression—an area of land that sinks below the surrounding land

diverse—made up of people from many different backgrounds

endangered—at risk of becoming extinct

fast—to eat little to nothing for a certain amount of time

Horn of Africa—a section of land in East Africa that sticks out into the Arabian Sea; Ethiopia, Somalia, Eritrea, and Djibouti make up the Horn of Africa.

hot springs—heated waters that flow up through cracks in the earth

Jesus Christ—the holy figure central to Christianity

landlocked—completely surrounded by land

monuments—structures that people build to remember important events or people

native—originating in a specific place

obelisks—tall, narrow structures with four sides that usually end in a pyramid shape at the top

pilgrimage—a religious journey that people make to a holy city or site

plateaus—areas of flat, raised land

sea level—the average level of the surface of the ocean

service jobs—jobs that perform tasks for people or businesses

textiles—fabrics or clothes that have been woven or knitted

tourists—people who travel to visit another country

tropical rain forests—thick, green forests that lie in the hot, wet regions near the equator

volcano—a hole in the earth; when a volcano erupts, hot, melted rock called lava shoots out.

To Learn More

AT THE LIBRARY

Bellward, Stacy. *Our First Amharic Words*. Minneapolis, Minn.: Amharic Kids, 2007.

Pohl, Kathleen. *Looking at Ethiopia*. Pleasantville, N.Y.: Gareth Stevens Pub., 2009.

Sheen, Barbara. *Foods of Ethiopia*. Detroit, Mich.: KidHaven Press, 2008.

ON THE WEB

Learning more about Ethiopia is as easy as 1, 2, 3.

1. Go to www.factsurfer.com.

2. Enter "Ethiopia" into the search box.

3. Click the "Surf" button and you will see a list of related Web sites.

With factsurfer.com, finding more information is just a click away.

Index

activities, 20

Addis Ababa, 4, 5

Aksum, 26

Blue Nile River, 7

capital (see Addis Ababa)

climate, 7, 10

daily life, 14-15

Dallol volcano, 8, 9

Danakil Desert, 7, 8-9

education, 16-17

Erta Ale volcano, 8

Ethiopian Highlands, 6, 7, 10

food, 22-23

Genna, 24

Great Rift Valley, 7, 11

holidays, 24-25

housing, 14, 15

Lalibela, 26, 27

landscape, 6-9

language, 13

location, 4-5

Meskel, 24

National Day, 24

people, 12-13, 20, 21

Ramadan, 25

sports, 21

Timkat, 24, 25

transportation, 15

wildlife, 10-11

working, 14, 16, 18-19

The images in this book are reproduced through the courtesy of: Tom Cockrem/Age Fotostock, front cover; Martin Zaick/Age Fotostock/SuperStock, p. 6; Cdkeyser, p. 7; Marka/SuperStock, p. 8; Prisma/ SuperStock, pp. 8-9; Sergey Gorshkov/Getty Images, pp. 10-11; Matej Hudovernik, p. 11 (top); Peter Betts, p. 11 (middle); Four Oaks, p. 11 (bottom); Joel Carillet/Getty Images, pp. 12-13; Joel Carillet/iStock, p. 14; Robert Harding Picture Library/SuperStock, p. 15; Sean Sprague/Age Fotostock/Superstock, pp. 16-17; Arno Jansen/iStock, p. 18; Thomas Cockrem/Alamy, p. 19 (left); Marcin Bartosz Czarnoleski, p. 19 (right); JENNY VAUGHAN/AFP/Getty Images/Newscom, p. 20; Juan Martinez, p. 21; Philippe Lissac/Newscom, p. 22; Otokimus, p. 23 (left); imagebroker.net/SuperStock, p. 23 (right); Andrew Heavens/Newscom, pp. 24-25; Andrew Holt/Getty Images, p. 26; Feije Riemersma, p. 27; Oleg Mit, p. 29.